From Grief to Grace

Images for Overcoming Sadness and Loss

Helen R. Lambin

ACTA
ASSISTING CHRISTIANS TO ACT
PUBLICATIONS

From Grief to Grace
Images for Overcoming Sadness and Loss
by Helen R. Lambin

Edited by Gregory F. Augustine Pierce
Cover Design by Tom A. Wright
Typesetting by Garrison Publications

Published by ACTA Publications
             Assisting Christians To Act
             4848 N. Clark Street
             Chicago, IL 60640
             800-397-2282

Library of Congress Catalog number: 96-80169

ISBN: 0-87946-154-3

Printed in the United States of America

00 99 98 97 96 5 4 3 2 1 First Printing

Table of Contents

To my loved ones
whose deaths showed me
that there can be
grace in grief.

Introduction

Images of Grief

"A picture is worth a thousand words."

This book is about grief; it is also about grace, because the one often follows the other. It is not intended to be a sad book. But it is intended to be a book for some of the dark hours of sadness and loss that come into our lives.

As a people of faith, we Christians know that we are an Easter people, people of the resurrection. We are on a journey that ends in joy. But our experience and, for that matter, our faith tell us that grief is also part of our daily lives. It is nothing we need to go looking for.

Our grief can take varied forms. It can come from many sources: the death of a loved one, the rupture of a vital relationship, the loss of a job and security, the pain experienced by those we love, family problems, the loss of health and independence, the slow or sudden demise of our dreams.

Grief cannot be easily or neatly defined so that everyone can instantly understand its meaning. One thing anyone who has ever experienced grief knows, however, is that you *know* grief when you *feel* grief.

Perhaps because grief is so difficult to capture in words, we use various ways to describe it—as if calling it by another name renders it somehow less alien, less overwhelming. For example, grief is frequently referred to as a "process." And it is a process, in the sense that it takes time and moves through various stages. But "process" is a rather abstract word that says little about the depth of the experience of grief. The word "process" can apply equally well to the making of potato chips or learning to ride a bike.

People also speak of grief as "work"—a kind of task to be completed. And it is that, too. There are things you have to work at in dealing with grief, so that it doesn't overwhelm you. But "work" doesn't quite describe the grief experience either. Work can be organized and sometimes delegated. Work can be a learning experience. Sometimes, if you're lucky, work can even be fun. Grief can, indeed, be a learning experience. But it is one job you cannot delegate. And no one could call it fun.

There is, of course, no one way to try to look at grief. We describe our grief in highly individual ways, because we are individuals. And we use a variety of resources, including our imaginations, to understand what we are experiencing.

One way of coming to grips with grief is by using images or symbols. We visualize or describe our grief by creating pictures or mental constructs that help us comprehend what is happening to us.

We use images in many areas of our lives, consciously and unconsciously. Christmas trees signal the birth of Christ, Easter lilies remind us of his resurrection. A circle with an angled line through a cigarette means "No Smoking," while one through a left or right arrow indicates "No Turns." Falling leaves signal us of the coming winter, and the first robins in cold climates remind us that spring is not far away.

Images can be a way of making something concrete, of serving as a kind of summary, of putting something into a form we can grasp, of offering reminders or warnings or encouragement. And images can be one way of beginning to deal with our grief and turn it into grace.

This book is divided into ten sections. Each section offers an image or two that can symbolize grief. They are not the only images of grief, of course. Symbols are like snowflakes—they are innumerable and no two are exactly alike. These offered here are a starting point. For any image or symbol to have meaning for you, you must develop it for yourself or in some way make it your own.

So in this book you will be asked to reflect on your own interpretations and feelings about various images. You will also be invited to create your own images. In other words, you will be asked to select and reflect on those images of grief that have meaning for you and might be or become images of grace for yourself and others.

Reflection

Circle some of the symbols of grief that have meaning for you now. Add as many others as you can.

Cross

Lily

Sunset

Dried Flowers

Bent Figure

Tears

Desert

Image ～～～～～～～～

Draw one of your significant images of grief.
(Don't worry about your artistic ability. No-
body but you need ever see this book.)

Image One

The Empty Tomb

"Hello darkness my old friend."

It is ironic that one of the major grief symbols of Christian faith and hope is based on apparent *emptiness*. It rests on something that isn't there, something someone expects to see and doesn't—the body of Jesus.

But the image of the empty tomb is also very appropriate. It is appropriate first of all because the Christian faith rests heavily on something that cannot be seen—except through the eyes of faith. "Blessed are you who have not seen, but have believed" (John 20:29). The image is appropriate because the sense of emptiness is such a profound part of the experience of grief.

All of the Gospels tell of the disciples' visit to the tomb, before they learn of the resurrection. But only John describes their sense of desolation, of bewilderment, of emptiness.

In Matthew, Mark and Luke, the disciples arrive at the tomb to be greeted immediately by an angel or angels, who announce that Jesus is risen. Jesus' followers are spared the experience of the empty tomb. In John's Gospel, however, the good news is a little slower in coming. Mary Magdalene and the other disciples learn of it the hard way—only after they encounter the terrible silence of the tomb in a hurried post-dawn visit.

In John, that most ethereal of Gospels, the story of the empty tomb is strikingly concrete (John 20:1-18). Early in the morning, Mary Magdalene goes to the tomb to help prepare Jesus' body for burial. (The disciples could not do this before because of the Sabbath, but also perhaps because of their own fear and sorrow.) But when she arrives, the tomb is empty, and the shock is overwhelming. Even the cold comfort of preparing Jesus' body for burial has been denied her.

Distraught, Mary runs off toward town to find Peter and "the other disciple...whom Jesus loved" to tell them: "They have taken the Lord out of the tomb, and we do not know where they have laid him."

There is a tremendous sense of urgency—a kind of frantic haste—in this part of the story. Mary "ran" to tell the disciples. The disciples "ran" to the tomb. Everyone, everything moves very quickly, driven by the need to accomplish something, to do something, without really knowing what it is they can or should do.

And this, too, is a part of the experience of grief in the first dark hours: the feeling that something has to be done, that there must be something that can be done—useful or not—to drown out the sounds of silence. And with all this frenetic activity comes the sense of futility that it doesn't seem to change anything—or even assuage our grief even a little.

The two other disciples, Peter and John, see the empty tomb, with the burial cloths lying there, and return to their homes. Not so Mary, who remains at the tomb, still weeping. It is only now, as she stops to look once again into the tomb, that she sees the two angels, who ask her why she is weeping. And it is only then that Jesus makes his presence known to his dear friend.

At first, Mary doesn't even recognize Jesus, even when he first speaks to her, and she mistakes him for a gardener. And small wonder. Theologians tell us that Mary encountered the risen Lord, who is very different from the Jesus she knew before.

But maybe that is not the only reason Mary did not recognize Jesus. It is very difficult to see clearly when you are in a state of grief. Everything and everyone that surrounds the grieving person looks somehow different from the way they did before. It is like seeing everything in black and white, instead of in color.

It is only when Jesus calls her by name, "Mary," that she at last recognizes him and realizes he is there, with her, in the space that seemed so empty just moments before. And it is only now, after she has truly experienced her loss, that Mary encounters the risen Lord.

The silence is suddenly filled with joy.

As Christians, we believe that Mary Magdalene's story is our story, that there certainly will come a time of healing and rejoicing. But for those who grieve, resurrection often comes about only after the terrible experience of not finding what we look for in the grey light of dawn, of discovering only sadness and confusion.

And, as with Mary, it is in our own places of silence that Jesus speaks to us with the promise that our emptiness will be filled.

Reflection ～～～～～～～～～

Where are some of the empty tombs in your life? What sounds of silences do you experience?

Image ~~~~~~~~~

Draw an image of emptiness or silence. What are you searching for to fill it? Draw that, too.

Image Two

The Dancing Figurine

"Dance, ballerina, dance. And do your
pirouettes in rhythm to your aching heart."

Few people are able to confront grief without some regrets. No matter how conscientiously we have tried to live our lives, no matter how loving we have been to others, there is always something we wish we had—or had not—done.

A certain amount of regret is humanizing and life-giving. It can be the seeds of growth and change that are part of life. Regret, however "regrettable," is a necessary part of growing, and growing up. Without it, we are condemned to endlessly repeat the same actions that bring pain to ourselves or others.

A *certain amount* of regret is humanizing and life-giving, that is. Too much regret, however, is paralyzing and deadening. Instead of dealing with the day we have, we become busy lamenting the ones behind. We regret all the things we could have achieved, all the mistakes we could have avoided, if only we knew then what we know now.

Such regret is like climbing aboard a music box for an endless ride while the music plays. In our grief we become a little porcelain music box figurine, endlessly turning on its little platform to an endless tune: "If only, if only, if only...."

Do you know this song? It is about all the things *done* or *said* you wish you hadn't. And worse, it is about all the things *undone* and *unsaid* you wish you had. (There is, fortunately for most of us, a sort of practical upper limit on our sins of *commission*. Twenty-four hours a day is just not enough time to make all the mistakes we're capable of, no matter how hard we try. But there is practically no limit on our sins of *omission*—the things we *should* have said or *should* have done.)

"If Only" is not the only song the music box of grief can play. It can also play such songs as: "What If?" and "Why Didn't?" and "Why Did This Have to Happen to Me (or Someone I Love)?" To ask these questions, to feel these regrets, is very human. But to keep circling atop a music box while waiting for answers that will never come is exhausting.

This particular music box can play—and the figurine can turn—endlessly. The little key at the bottom can constantly rewind itself, and the music need never run down. So the poor little figure never gets any respite...and for that matter never goes anywhere. Around and around its circle of regrets it goes, while the music tinkles away: "If only, if only, if only...."

There are very probably things we should have done or left undone. Some things might have been better if we had acted differently. But some things might have been worse. We can only know the consequences of the choices we make, not of the ones we don't make.

How fortunate that God is more forgiving of us than we are! God does not tell us: "Pick up that untidy bundle of regrets and get on top of that music box and start turning." Instead we are told: "Blessed are those who mourn, for they shall be comforted" (Matthew 5:4) and "Come to me, all who labor and are heavy laden, and I will give you rest" (Matthew 11:28). And that rest includes a reprieve from the burden of dancing to the "If Onlies."

Music boxes can be enchanting toys for adults or children. But they are not supposed to be role models for managing our grief. At some point we need to stop the music and step off the box. Only that stops the key from turning and allows the song to run down.

Then, in the restful silence, we can choose to play a different song.

Reflection ∿∿∿∿∿∿∿∿

What songs does *your* music box play? What
song or songs would you *like* to hear?

Image ~~~~~~~~~~~

Draw your music box, complete with figurine and the key that turns it on and off.

Post-It Notes and Tiny Whispers

"The Lord was not in the earthquake."

There is nothing small about grief. The event that lies behind it always looms very large. And grief casts a giant shadow.

But the everyday events that bring our grief crashing back to our consciousness at unexpected times tend to be such small things:
a fragment of music,
the smell of baking bread,
a souvenir bought on a long ago vacation,
a coffee mug used at a workplace,
a storybook once read and reread to a child,
a flash of color turning a distant corner,
curtains blowing in an open window,
a place you once lived,
the whistle of a distant train.

The list could go on and on. There they are—sticky, colorful little tags of memory, demanding our attention: "Remember when..."; "Doesn't this remind you of..."; "Things used to be...." They are Post-It Notes from our grief.

Person after person has spoken of the impact of little things that recall grief with the force of a blow to the heart. These often come like the sudden return of a summer storm, just when it had appeared to subside.

On the other hand, it can be very hard to see signs of God's presence at times of grief, loss or profound discouragement. Yet this is often when we are most apt to seek it. But because we seek God so desperately, God can at times be desperately hard to find. It is rather like trying to open a locked car door on a cold day when you're in a hurry— because your fingertips keep brushing past the key in your pocket or purse.

God's presence does not necessarily come in the way we expect it or in a way that can't be missed. Hollywood miracles are unmistakable, awesome spectaculars with thunder and lightening courtesy of the Department of Special Effects. Real life works differently. Miracles are not necessarily dramatic. More often they are quiet whispers that we can miss if we are not listening for them.

Grief can only be lived one day at a time, otherwise its weight becomes unbearable. But grief cannot be lived twenty-four hours a day, seven days a week. We need to take some kind of breaks—a series of brief holidays from grief. Sometimes it may be an entire day, more often the odd hour. And sometimes it may come down to minutes. But one way or another, we need to set aside some kind of time in which we say, "For *this* hour, or for *these* moments, I will not mourn. I will do something that I enjoy, however small and ordinary."

And it is most often in small things, in small ways, that the process of healing begins:

a cup of coffee on a summer morning,
a phone call from—or to—a friend,
the smile of a child,
a good book or movie,
a walk in the woods,

the company of a pet,
chicken soup or other foods from childhood,
an act of kindness—given or received,
a quiet (or painful) moment of prayer.

These are all tiny whispers that begin to overcome the Post-It Notes from Our Grief and help us to rediscover the loving presence of God.

Consider, for example, what happened to the prophet Elijah in the cave at Horeb (I Kings 19). Elijah is resting in the cave, in flight for his life after a hostile (on both sides) encounter with the prophets of Baal. Elijah is discouraged and the presence of the Lord seems remote. Suddenly he is told by an angel to go outside, that the Lord will be passing by. Here comes now the Special Effects: "A strong and heavy wind was rending the mountains and crushing rocks before the Lord...." Now that *is* dramatic.

But it is also not where Elijah encounters the presence of the Lord.

The story continues: "After the wind there was an earthquake—but the Lord was not in the earthquake. After the earthquake there was fire—but the Lord was not in the fire. After the fire there was a tiny whispering sound. When he heard this, Elijah hid his face in his cloak...."

Thunder and lightening and mighty winds are hard to ignore, just as are the Post-It Notes from Our Grief. Sometimes you have to listen very carefully, however, for the tiny whispers that indicate that God is truly near.

Reflection ～～～～～～～～～

If you could have one small, quiet miracle in your life, what would it be? What tiny whisper have you heard—or ignored—today?

Image 〜〜〜〜〜〜〜〜〜

Write one or more Post-It Notes from your grief. Then write a Post-It Note back to your grief.

Image Four

Salvage and Saving Grace

"Life keeps on happening."

*L*ife isn't fair. It isn't necessarily neat or easy, either.

In times of grief we need support from those around us, from others significant in our lives. That doesn't make the pain go away, of course, but it does help us endure the process. Professional therapists recommend seeking help from others. So do popular advice columnists.

The trouble is that, while we're trying to get on with our lives, other people are also trying to get on with *theirs*. Which means that the people around us, the people we need support from, also may well need support, understanding, encouragement, approval from us.

It can be very hard to be supportive of someone else when we're awash with grief ourselves. There is only one thing harder than being needed by others when we're already in need ourselves, however, and that is not to be needed at all.

One image that may help us turn our grief into grace is that of *salvage*. Salvage is what is saved from a wreckage that might possibly be useful to someone or something, someplace or somewhere. Salvage is, if you will, a kind of "saving" grace. We take something that ordinarily would be destroyed or wasted and we sort it out and save it in a way that might be shared or reused.

Can we salvage our grief?

Years ago, on one of the popular soap operas (still running today) there was a character called Grandpa Hughes, who was a kindly wisdom figure. Other people would quote him, especially one particular saying: "Well, as Grandpa Hughes says, 'Life keeps on happening.' "

The actor who played Grandpa Hughes died. He had become so identified with the role and so beloved in it by audience and fellow actors alike, however, that he could not be replaced. His character was killed off the show, but for a long time the phrase lingered in times of crisis: "Well, as Grandpa Hughes used to say, 'Life keeps on happening.' "

Despite their grief over the loss of their friend, the writers of that show had salvaged Grandpa Hughes and his saying in the service of the continuation of life.

As a people of faith, we believe in trying to salvage our experiences. Painful experiences are not easily biodegradable. They are *there*, filling our field of vision, seemingly impervious to rain, wind and time.

Because they are *there*, one way or another they are going to leave their traces. We can't eliminate them. But we do have a voice in deciding what form they will take.

It seems such a pity to waste them. It is hard enough to experience grief, still more difficult not to learn from it and to share what we've learned.

We all know people who have become

bent and embittered by grief. We can understand them, sympathize with them, and often identify with them—but only from a distance. We also tend to avoid them, because their despair can begin to diminish our own hope or add to our own hopelessness.

We also know people who have somehow managed not only to survive grief, but to have in some sense been strengthened by it—to have grown in compassion, understanding, faith. These are the true Easter people, who are experiencing here and now the beginnings of resurrection and rebirth. We may admire them, envy them, and perhaps wonder how they do it. We can also draw from them, without taking anything away from them, their sense of hope.

We can't stop life from happening, still less change what has already happened. Unless we avoid love and commitment completely, we cannot avoid grief. But we do have a say in deciding whether we will let it consume us, or whether it will become a part of our own rebirth and a saving grace for others.

As Grandpa Hughes used to say, "Life keeps on happening."

Reflection ～～～～～～～

What is one of the things you can salvage from your grief? How can you be a saving grace for others?

Image ∾∾∾∾∾∾∾∾∾

Draw a billboard or a truck panel with lettering for your salvage company.

Image Five

Slag Heaps and Heather

"The heather on the hill."

In the mining country of South Wales, slag heaps still stand, stark reminders of the past. They remain from the time when coal fueled industry and miners descended daily into the depths of the earth in darkness lit only by lamps.

Beyond the mountains, however, the Welsh land is very different. There the hills are green, fresh and tree-covered. Even the famous moors, treeless and rolling, are bright with purple heather and yellow gorse. Flocks of sheep graze and stray across the winding roads and among the bushes and tall ferns.

But not so in the mining region. There the moors are browner, more barren—beautiful in their way, but much bleaker. And there tower the slag heaps, huge black piles of discarded coal cinder. The mines are closed now—seams of coal were exhausted, alternative sources of fuel were found, certain mines were determined to be unprofitable. The closure was both good news and bad. The good news was that the miners no longer had to take the cage ride to their work in the dark earth—work that brought danger and disease particular to those who worked in the mines. The bad news was that with the mines went the jobs that sustained the people who lived in the plain cottage row houses pictured in Richard Llewellyn's book, and later the film, *How Green Was My Valley.*

But the slag heaps remain, buffeted by wind and rain and snow as the seasons come and go. They stand there—ominous, lifeless and sometimes deadly. On occasion they have been known to shift position in a kind of slag slide, as in the town of Aberffan, where the dead included children trapped in a local school.

And yet, as the slag heaps blot the landscape decade after decade, they gradually begin to change. Shoots of new grass start to grow up their sides—brownish grass, like that on the surrounding moors, but still grass. And here and there appear a few shoots of purple or white heather, a flash of color among the black. Further down the road, at the edge of a small, brown, man-made lake formed by waters used by a former iron smeltery, families picnic and children and small dogs play along the shore, oblivious to the slag heaps in the distance. It is as though Mother Nature has begun the process of recycling. She is exercising her saving grace of once again bringing life and hope out of the most unexpected places.

In time, perhaps, the rains and snows will compress the slag heaps enough that they can no longer shift. And in time, perhaps, the grass and the heather will reclaim them com-pletely, so that those who see them will ob-serve only small hills that seem to stand out little from the others.

For many of us, our grief is like huge, abandoned slag heaps, blotting our land-scapes, reminding us of better times. Some-times they too can shift and slide, destroying everything in their path and stilling all life. But mostly they just stand there, reminders of

seams of dreams that ran out or proved un-
workable, markers of losses buried deep, of
regrets too heavy to move, too big to ignore.

Yet even a slag heap of grief will in time
show signs of life—some shoots of compassion
here, a spring of hope there. Such a grief may
never disappear completely, but it may become part of a larger landscape where
growth begins to appear in unexpected
places.

Reflection ～～～～～～～～

Have you seen any signs of life or growth amidst your grief? What are they and how do you react to them?

Image 〜〜〜〜〜〜〜〜〜

Draw a picture of your grief, with whatever grows on it or goes on around it.

Image Six

A Labor of Love

"Take a deep, cleansing breath."

Tolstoy said, "All happy families are alike. Every unhappy family is unhappy in its own way." In one sense the same might be said of grief. No two people experience grief in precisely the same way. And no two experiences of grief are exactly alike. Nor is grief exactly like any other experience.

And yet in the experience of grief is the faint, firm echo of another experience of upheaval and change, an experience (ironically enough) that appears its precise opposite: a pregnant woman's experience of labor.

This may seem a strange image, a mixed-up sort of metaphor. What do grief and labor have in common?

First of all, both involve periods of seemingly unbearable pain. In both grief and labor, the type, duration and degree of pain varies from individual to individual, situation to situation. Expectant mothers are taught ways of dealing with and lessening the pain, just as books like this one describe techniques for dealing with grief. But few who have experienced either childbirth or serious grief would describe it as pain free!

Like labor pain, the pain of grief does, at some points, come and go—or at least intensify and subside. Unlike labor pain, however, the pain of grief is not predictable. It does not come and go at rhythmic, regular intervals, with contractions of a certain duration leading to a final, climatic release. But, as everyone who's experienced it knows, grief, too, has a rhythm and timing of its own.

With grief, as with labor, there is the feeling of sheer helplessness. You can't organize it or decide to simply get busy with something else and hope it will go away. As with labor pain, it is hard to really relax, still less enjoy, the moments of respite between the pangs of grief, because you're constantly on guard against the next episode.

During both grief and labor, it can be extraordinarily hard to concentrate on anything else. We all know people who iron while watching the news, catch up on paper work while waiting for the dentist, or fold the laundry or polish the kitchen floor while they talk on the phone. Some situations, however, don't lend themselves very well to multiple activities. It is hard to settle down with a good book if we are waiting for an important, longed-for, long-distance phone call. It is next to impossible to concentrate on studying after hearing a strange noise in the basement.

So it is with labor, so too with grief. While in early labor, a woman may decide to read or knit or watch TV. But in later labor, as the pains grow stronger and the birth comes closer, she is not interested in much of anything else. A person who is grieving is likewise unlikely to want to do other things. (With times of grief, at least in our society, however, you are not only expected to get on with your life, it may be demanded of you by family obligations, jobs, financial responsibilities, or many other day-to-day concerns.)

Finally, with both grief and labor our lives are in some way forever changed.

Grief is, of course, labor of a very different type. There isn't the long-anticipated joyous outcome to look forward to, no crib to buy or borrow, no layette to lovingly prepare. There aren't standard, visible bodily changes, although changes there may be. And no one says congratulations to you on your new state. Instead, there are words of sympathy, if anyone says anything at all.

And people may not say anything at all. For some reason, a state of grief is like a pregnancy that people consider awkward. They don't know quite how to deal with it— whether to look for appropriate words or just pretend they don't notice and assume that in time it will go away.

The most significant difference between labor and grief, of course, is that there is no long-awaited little person to cradle after the pain. But there is, in one sense, a new person, a somewhat different person, perhaps even a very different person to be comforted—and that person is the griever. Grief can make us more compassionate and caring, or we can become colder and more wary. But in the process of grief we change in one way or another, for better or for worse, and we must be attentive to ourselves.

If we are to survive intense grief and go on living and loving, rather than simply existing, we need to go through a kind of birth process. Because what there is, what there can be, and what there must be to survive is another kind of birth, the birth—or rebirth—of ourselves.

Thus does grief become a labor of love.

Reflection ～～～～～～～～～

Whom do you see as the "newness" that will be born of your own labor of love? Where would you like your grief to lead?

Image 〰〰〰〰〰〰〰〰〰

Draw the person you hope to give birth to.
Include whatever background elements or
props you think necessary.

Image Seven

The Long Distance Call

"I just called to say, 'I love you.'"

This book is for those who grieve, whatever the reason. There is no one source of grief. All grief is a labor of love, because we are mourning the loss of that which we cherished—a person, a marriage, a job, a home, a dream. But this particular section is about a particular kind of loss—the death of someone we loved.

In one sense, death is the complete reversal of the birth process. Throughout the months of pregnancy, there is another person who is an integral part of the mother—a person who cannot ordinarily be seen, still less heard, but who can be felt. There are fluttery fist clenchings, lively little kicks, and suspected somersaults.

But shortly before the onset of labor, the baby's intrauterine activity often appears to diminish. After the months of feeling fetal activity, this feels strange, uneasy. "Is he all right?" parents-to-be wonder. "What is going on with her now?" they ask anxiously. Before the fetus begins its major journey down the birth canal, there is a sort of silence from within. It is, to mix metaphors, a sort of lull before the storm—a brief period of waiting before the new person who, after nine months time, will finally make himself or herself seen—and heard—at last.

With the process of bereavement, on the contrary, we begin with a person who has been seen and heard over and over, again and again, day after day, month after month, year after year. Then, suddenly, that person's activity ceases.

We listen for the voice that can no longer be heard. We have so much to say that can't be said. If we experience something funny, interesting, unnerving, we think, "Just wait until I tell...." Then we remember, once again, that our loved one is no longer there to tell—or to respond.

We think to ourselves: If only we could talk just one more time, to say the things we left unsaid, repeat what we did say, or ask the questions we forgot to ask. If only we could make one last, very long-distance call.

And yet, at odd moments, at quiet moments, we sense that those we loved are still with us. They are in our memories, in our stories, in our hearts, our minds, our souls. We even swear that at times we feel their "movements" in our lives. Sometimes their presence is exciting, joyous, profound. Sometimes it simply makes us sad, because it reminds us how we miss them.

Like the aftermath of labor, we are dealing with another person present now, but in a wholly different way, in a sort of mirror image of the birth process. Before, the person we loved was a part of our external environment. Now he or she has in one sense moved within us, and with the change there comes lack of sight and sound.

As Christians, we believe in the Communion of Saints. We announce this formally in our creed; we express it ritually in our liturgy; we show it architecturally in our shrines.

But for many of us the belief in a life hereafter is still more or less a theological abstraction which has little relevance to daily life. Or it is something we learned as children that we put away with the things of a child.

Which is a pity. The Communion of Saints is much more concrete than a theological abstraction and much more adult than the memorized words of childhood. What it means is that the bonds of love—however stretched and intangible they are—outlast this life. We believe that our loved ones are really, truly, actively alive and, what is more, are present to us in some holy, miraculous, wonderful way. In one sense, we believe that we can make that ultimate long-distance call anytime we want—and that it will be answered.

This is not, of course, enough to take away our grief. Telephone calls are not a substitute for being physically present. But it is better than nothing, at least for now, until the circle is closed.

The pain of labor is not the end of the birth process; the end is life itself. Christians know that the pain of grief is not the end of the process of grieving. The end is, ultimately, in the resurrection—in our resurrection, in the resurrection of those we love.

Reflection 〜〜〜〜〜〜〜〜〜

Write the script for that one long-distance call
you wish you could make. Be sure to write
both parts of the conversation.

Image ∽∽∽∽∽∽∽∽∽

Draw a picture of your understanding of the Communion of Saints. Place your loved ones in the picture.

Image Eight

The Prisoners

"Stone walls do not a prison make,
nor iron bars a cage."

In the Academia Museum in Florence, Italy, stands Michelangelo's statue of David. "Stands" is used loosely. Actually, David looks as if he is about to step off his pedestal any moment. Confident, alert, eyes fixed on the distant and invisible Goliath, the statue dominates the room.

So compelling is David that at first you don't notice the pieces of unfinished sculpture that lead to it—great blocks of marble with partially sculpted figures emerging head and shoulders from their base. These are Michelangelo's famous *Prisoners*.

Michelangelo's theory about sculpture was that the figures are already *there*, in the stone, waiting to be shaped. All you had to do was strip away all that wasn't part of the form "imprisoned" within the marble. The Prisoners never quite made it completely. The project they were commissioned for (a tomb for Pope Julius II) was changed, and the Prisoners were never freed from their marble prisons. Some are more finished than others. One unhappy-looking Prisoner, in particular, looks as if he could and would escape if someone would just give him a hand.

There is something very sad about the Prisoners, trapped for all time in their marble blocks. It can't be much fun sitting around waist-deep in a block of stone, while Bermuda-clad tourists wander by, indifferent to your plight.

Grief can make *us* prisoners. We may not be made of stone, but we can feel like it—frozen, cold, unable to move or change position—while the rest of the world walks by, oblivious to what we are going through.

Unlike Michelangelo's Prisoners, however, we have a choice in liberating ourselves. It isn't an overnight project, but little by little—a shift here, a chipping away there—we can try to wiggle free of the blocks that hold us. People around us can help, too—a tug here, a push there, or maybe just offering some support to help keep our balance as we take our first steps.

And unlike the Prisoners in Florence, we have easy and ongoing access to the original Creator to help us get on with the job. Unlike Michelangelo, our Creator doesn't get so distracted by other jobs that there isn't time to finish ours.

Freeing ourselves from our grief is not easy. We may have to do it in steps. Sometimes we may have to rework our original image of ourself and try a different creative approach so that our true, post-grief self can emerge.

But it's better than remaining a prisoner. And, like Michelangelo's David, the finished product will be a work of art.

Reflection ～～～～～～～～～

What are some of the tools you could use to chip away at your prison? What is the new image of yourself that lies imbedded in your grief?

Image 〜〜〜〜〜〜〜〜〜〜

Draw your prison. Then map out your escape route, including the people who could help you.

Image Nine

Unseen Beads and Pre-Prayed Prayers

"But deliver us from evil. Amen."

The Rosary is out of favor, part of the "old church." But it's coming back with the growing interest in Eastern religions. The Rosary has been described as the great Christian mantra, special words of meditation, repeated over and over again, to achieve tranquility and enlightenment. And so it may be. For generations, the Rosary has been a prayer many said in times of the heavy darkness of grief.

People who do have rosaries often tend to have more than one. They are given them as gifts, brought back from journeys, passed on from family and friends. But equally often, people don't make a point of admitting they pray the Rosary, because of the stereotype that has come to be attached to owning a pair of "beads," as they used to be called. That stereotype is of a little old woman, head wrapped in a scarf, fingering her beads with work-hardened hands, ignoring all around her.

So Rosary sayers often stay anonymous. Stereotypes are uncomfortable—especially being made into one.

Louise has four rosaries, each of which has a meaning for her. The little blue plastic one belonged to one of her children and reminds her of the days when she could repair the entire world with a cookie, a story, a hug. The worn, black one belonged to her mother, and before that, to her father. The sparkling green crystal rosary was bought by a teen-age son with money earned working nights in a rectory fielding phone calls for sleeping clergy. The fourth, of pale blue glass, belonged to her sister and was given to her during a particularly difficult time of grief.

"I can't even pray," Louise told her sister. "I'm too confused; I don't have the energy; I don't even know where to start."

At their next encounter, her sister gave Louise the used rosary. "It is pre-prayed," she explained—sounding rather like a used-car salesman pointing out one of the older models. "So it's easier to use. It's not like one that has to be broken in."

Louise didn't really understand her sister then. But still, she accepted the rosary, rambling her way through the decades each night until she fell asleep. Somehow, the pre-prayed rosary *was* easier to use.

True, there are times when used prayers won't do. Usually, we are encouraged to pray from our hearts, in our own words, or even without words. But there are times, in-cluding times of grief (perhaps *especially* in times of grief) when used prayers come into their own. We need the familiar phrases, the words that come without groping for them, the comfort of the prayers learned long ago or at least at a quieter time.

Fortunately, God does not demand eloquence from us, any more than we de-mand it from *our* children.

One Ash Wednesday not long ago, Louise encountered one of the dreaded rosary stereotypes. There the woman was—short, stocky, wearing a babushka, looking uncertainly from pew to pew. She caught Louise's eye and sat down next to her.

Throughout the first part of the liturgy, the woman prayed the Rosary. Louise couldn't so much see it as hear it—the dreaded sibilant ss's, repeated for five long decades. Not terribly loud, but too loud for Louise to ignore. Louise tried not to grow impatient and give the woman a chilling stare. After all, it was Ash Wednesday. But as they approached the Prayer of the Faithful, Louise could not resist glancing over to see how much farther the old woman had to go.

The look didn't help much. Yes, the woman's hands were in position, stretched out at approximately a decade apart; her fingers moved, counting. But Louise couldn't see any rosary, because the woman wasn't holding one. There she sat, praying her invisible rosary, from long habit able to finger the beads that weren't there.

Of course, it is possible that the woman held a very small, obscure set of beads that Louise just didn't see. But Louise doesn't think so, and prefers not to think so. Somehow the idea of a small, elderly woman calmly saying her prayers on unseen beads is an image that gave Louise much comfort in her own grief.

Much of our faith depends on that which cannot be seen and cannot be felt.

Baron Tweedsmuir (John Buchan) defined an atheist as "someone who has no invisible means of support."

The little old woman in the babushka would have understood that.

Reflection ~~~~~~~~~~

What are some of your invisible means of support? Which pre-prayed prayers do you find especially comforting? Pray them now.

Image 〜〜〜〜〜〜〜〜

Draw a set of beads and color them with all the different colors that you feel.

Image Ten

"Our Willie"

"Memories, misty water-colored memories."

In a small town in the middle of Iowa there is an old cemetery set in the hills. It is old, at any rate, for that part of the Midwest. Here are the tombstones, barely legible, of a handful of people born in the late seventeen hundreds. Here, too, are clusters of graves for the Civil War veterans, various family plots, and the sudden additions for a long-forgotten epidemic.

There is such a sense of peace about the place, a glimpse of history, a feeling of continuity. One of the headstones is marked "Our Willie."

Willie's tombstone lies near the foot of a tree beside the narrow gravel road that winds through the oldest and most remote part of the cemetery. It is a medium-sized, rectangular headstone—thick, solid and weathered. On it are simply the words, "Our Willie," the name of his parents, and "aged three years." On top of the stone is carved a small stone dog, curved at rest, head on paws, waiting for his master to awaken to play once again.

No one now can tell who Willie was or what illness or accident cut his life so short. The stone is worn by the rains and winds and snows of nearly a century. Yet someone, perhaps a stranger, still remembers his grave. Each summer he or she leaves a pot of red flowers at the foot of the marker—bright and colorful petals that a child would like.

Those who loved and lost Willie—his parents, grandparents, brothers and sisters— must have long since joined Willie in the king-dom of love and light. Perhaps—depending on your theology—the little dog, too, is there with him, rewarded for his fidelity.

Whoever Willie was, he didn't have much time to leave his mark on the world. But he must have left his mark on people's hearts. There is something about the stone that still speaks of it. It does not say "William" and his surname, with the formal date of birth and death. It says "Our Willie...aged three years." You have the feeling that Willie was greatly loved and that each of his days counted to his loved ones.

As we struggle with our own grief, perhaps we need to give it our own, personalized "tombstone," one that captures our true feelings of loss and sadness—a message that we can send down the years into the future to let others know how much we hurt, how much we cared.

Reflection ～～～～～～～～

What memories of your loss do you always want to keep? Begin to write them down.

Image ⌒⌒⌒⌒⌒⌒⌒⌒⌒⌒

Draw the tombstone for your grief. Inscribe it with the words and symbols meaningful only to you.

Also Available From
ACTA Publications

The New Day Journal
A Journey from Grief to Healing
by Sr. Mauryeen O'Brien, O.P.

A book offering those who have lost a loved one a
structured way to work through the "tasks of grief,"
including accepting the reality of the loss, experiencing the pain of grief, adjusting to the new environment in which the deceased is missing, and moving
on with life. 92 page workbook, $8.95.

The Death of a Wife
Reflections for a Grieving Husband
by Robert L. Vogt

A collection of poignant reflections for any husband
mourning the death of his wife. Each of the thirty-one
brief stories, remembrances, meditations and poems
considers a different facet of the grieving process.
112 pages, $8.95.

The Legend of the Bells and Other Tales
Stories of the Human Spirit
by John Shea

Twenty-five of theologian and master storyteller John Shea's favorite stories, including "The Grieving Woman and the Spiritual Master." Drawn from many different religious traditions, spiritual legends, and everyday experiences, each story speaks directly to the spiritual seeker's heart and mind and is followed by Shea's thought-provoking explanation, which gives a practical, personal relevance to the story. 192 pages, $12.95.

The Rosary and *The Stations of the Cross*
produced by Sheldon Cohen

These traditional devotions are available on both audio and video tape. Original meditations and music, performed by professional vocalists and musicians, have made these beautiful tapes a source of comfort and inspiration for many. *The Rosary*—70 minutes, audio $9.95, CD $14.95, video $19.95. *The Stations of the Cross*—40 minutes, audio $8.95, video $19.95.

AVAILABLE FROM BOOKSELLERS OR CALL
800-397-2282.